D1472166

XTREME SNAKES
MAMBAS

BY S.L. HAMILTON

A&D Xtreme
An imprint of Abdo Publishing | abdopublishing.com

abdopublishing.com

Published by Abdo Publishing, a division of ABDO, PO Box 398166, Minneapolis, Minnesota 55439. Copyright ©2019 by Abdo Consulting Group, Inc. International copyrights reserved in all countries. No part of this book may be reproduced in any form without written permission from the publisher. A&D Xtreme™ is a trademark and logo of Abdo Publishing.

Printed in the United States of America, North Mankato, MN.
022018
092018

Editor: John Hamilton
Copy Editor: Bridget O'Brien
Graphic Design: Sue Hamilton
Cover Design: Candice Keimig and Pakou Moua
Cover Photo: iStock
Interior Photos & Illustrations: Alamy-pgs 22-23 & 28-29;
Galileo Ramos-pgs 6-7; Getty-pgs 10-11, 16-17, 24-25 & 26-27;
iStock-pg 1; Minden Pictures-pgs 4-5, 18-19 & 20-21;
Science Source-pgs 14-15; Shutterstock-pgs 2-3, 7 (inset), 8-9, 12-13, 30-31 & 32.

Library of Congress Control Number: 2017963892
Publisher's Cataloging-in-Publication Data
Names: Hamilton, S.L., author.
Title: Mambas / by S.L. Hamilton.
Description: Minneapolis, Minnesota : Abdo Publishing, 2019. |
    Series: Xtreme snakes | Includes online resources and index.
Identifiers: ISBN 9781532116025 (lib.bdg.) | ISBN 9781532156953 (ebook)
Subjects: LCSH: Mambas--Juvenile literature. | Poisonous snakes--Juvenile
    literature. | Snakes--Juvenile literature. | Reptiles--Juvenile literature. |
    Herpetology--Juvenile literature.
Classification: DDC 597.964--dc23

CONTENTS

MAMBAS

Mambas are one of the most feared snakes in their homeland of Africa. These sleek serpents can lift half their body off the ground. Since some grow to a length of up to 14 feet (4 m), that means an attack on a human is sometimes face-to-face. Two drops of mamba venom in a human means death, often within an hour. Luckily, mambas do not want anything to do with humans. Unless trapped or threatened, mambas prefer to simply stay as far away from people as possible.

*Eastern
Green Mamba*

BODY PARTS

There are four species of mambas: black, eastern green, western green, and Jameson's. Their scientific genus name, *Dendroaspis*, means "tree asp."

Streamlined, coffin-shaped head

Hollow, needle-like fangs that stay fixed in place.

Separate lower jaw sections allow the mouth to open wide over prey.

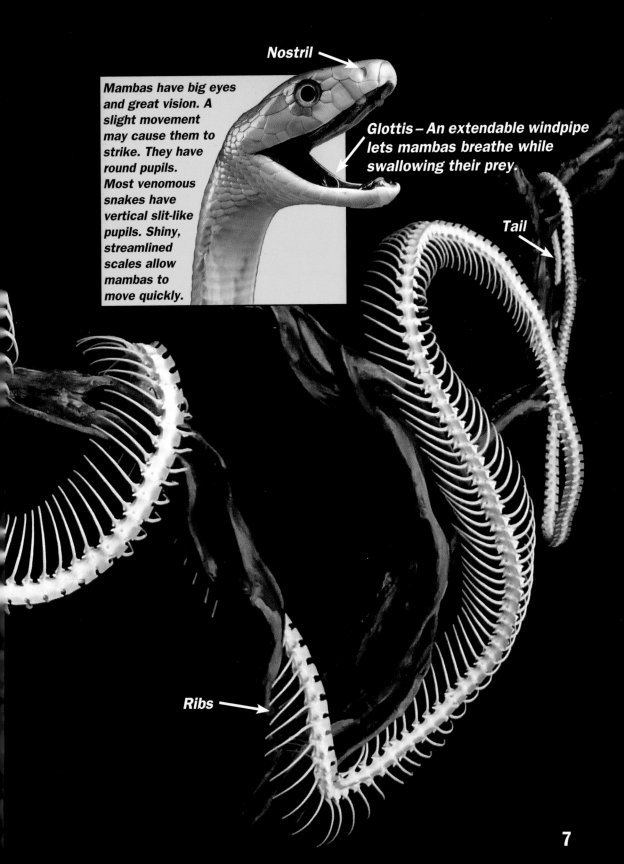

Nostril

Mambas have big eyes and great vision. A slight movement may cause them to strike. They have round pupils. Most venomous snakes have vertical slit-like pupils. Shiny, streamlined scales allow mambas to move quickly.

Glottis – An extendable windpipe lets mambas breathe while swallowing their prey.

Tail

Ribs

Fangs and Venom

Mamba fangs are short, hollow, and fixed in place. They are located far forward in the mamba's jaw and do not fold up. This design, together with incredibly quick striking speed, allows the snakes to nick fast-moving prey. Only a tiny amount of venom is needed to kill.

Mamba venom is a neurotoxin. The venom stops the brain from sending instructions to the body. Within minutes, the victim is unable to move. The heart stops beating and the lungs stop working. Antivenin is needed to save someone bitten by a mamba.

PREY AND HUNTING

Mambas are stalkers and ambush predators. Their large eyes find prey. They then wait for their chance to strike. Since they can climb trees, they often eat birds. They also eat rodents and other small mammals, as well as other snakes. Mambas bite and allow their venom to kill their prey, and then swallow it whole, head first.

XTREME FACT – A mamba can eat prey up to four times the size of its head.

HABITAT

Mambas live in eastern and southern Africa. They are excellent tree climbers, and often make their homes high above the ground. With their excellent camouflage, they easily hunt birds for prey. Mambas also live in lairs on the ground or in rocky crevices. They often take abandoned burrows or termite mounds as homes.

XTREME FACT – Mambas are excellent swimmers.

NESTING

Mambas lay 10 to 17 eggs in an underground nest or a hollow tree. Mothers stay with the nest until the brood hatches.

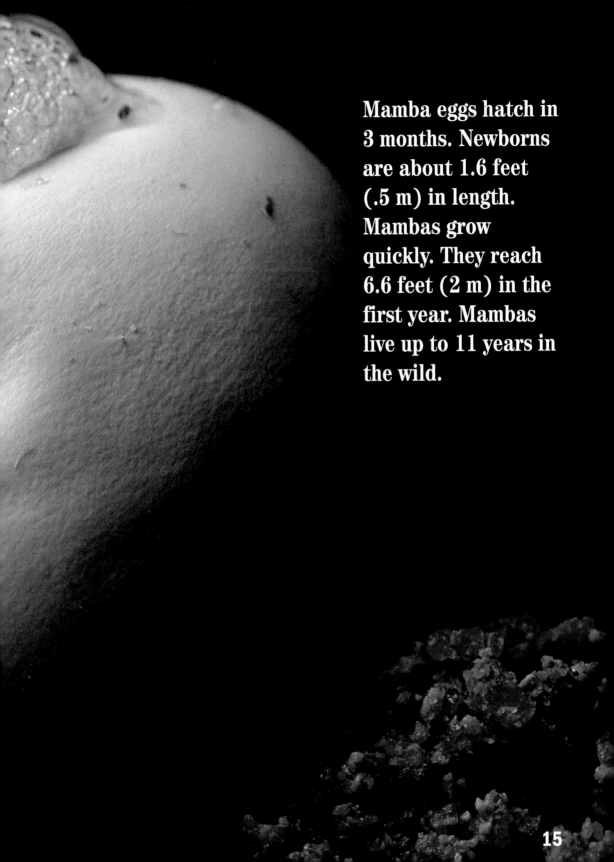

Mamba eggs hatch in 3 months. Newborns are about 1.6 feet (.5 m) in length. Mambas grow quickly. They reach 6.6 feet (2 m) in the first year. Mambas live up to 11 years in the wild.

BLACK MAMBAS

Black mambas are the second-longest venomous snake. They average 6.6 feet (2 m) in length, but can grow as long as 14 feet (4 m). Only king cobras are longer. Black mambas are actually grey to dark brown in color, with white bellies. Their black mouths give them their name.

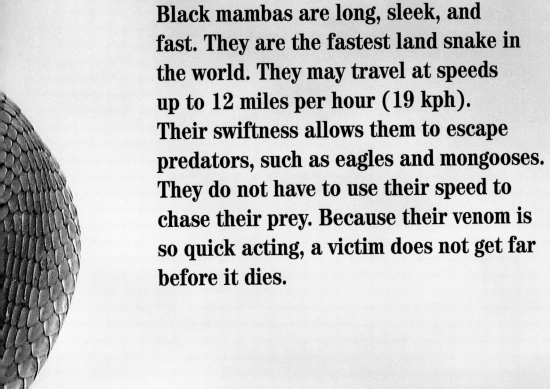

Black mambas are long, sleek, and fast. They are the fastest land snake in the world. They may travel at speeds up to 12 miles per hour (19 kph). Their swiftness allows them to escape predators, such as eagles and mongooses. They do not have to use their speed to chase their prey. Because their venom is so quick acting, a victim does not get far before it dies.

XTREME FACT – Mamba poop smells like curry powder.

EASTERN GREEN MAMBAS

Eastern green mambas are the smallest mamba species. They live in the eastern forests of southern Africa. They grow to an average of 5.9 to 6.6 feet (1.8 to 2 m) long. The largest green mambas may grow up to 8.2 feet (2.5 m).

Eastern green mambas are tree dwellers. Their glossy green coloring is excellent camouflage. Although active during the day, they are rarely seen. They usually remain in the treetops, only going to the ground to get fallen prey. They eat birds, eggs, small reptiles, and small mammals.

XTREME FACT – The eastern green mamba's venom is one-tenth as deadly as a black mamba's.

WESTERN GREEN MAMBAS

Like their eastern cousins, western green mambas are also treetop dwellers. They are found in the woods and rainforests of western Africa. They grow 4.6 feet (1.4 m) to 6.9 feet (2.1 m) in length. The longest-known western green mamba reached 7.9 feet (2.4 m).

XTREME FACT – Mambas have very strong stomach acid. They digest nearly all of the animals they eat, but may poop out small bits of bones, feathers, beaks, and hair. It takes about 8 to 10 hours for prey to be digested.

Western green mambas drop from high tree branches onto their prey of birds, lizards, eggs, and small mammals. They often bite and release their prey. Their fast-acting venom quickly stops the heart and breathing of the victim. The snake does not have far to go to collect its dinner.

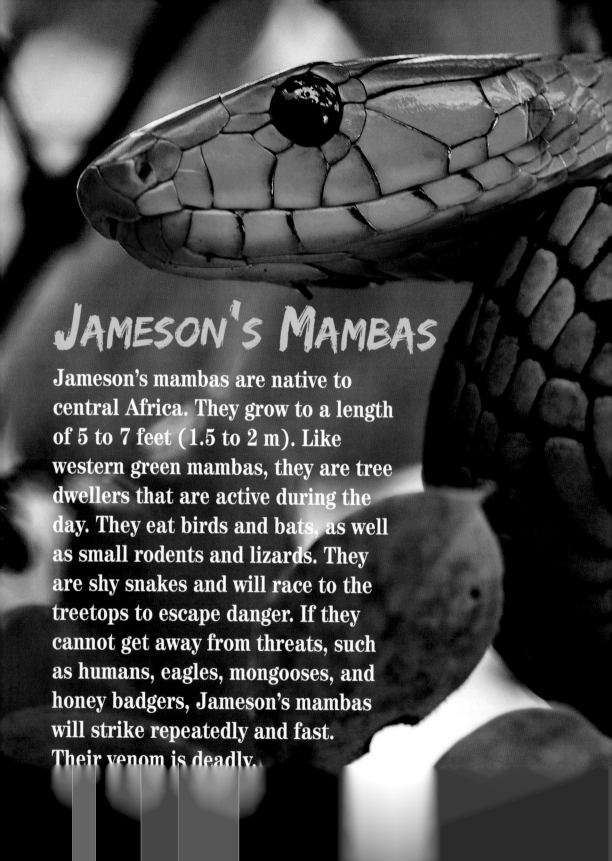

JAMESON'S MAMBAS

Jameson's mambas are native to central Africa. They grow to a length of 5 to 7 feet (1.5 to 2 m). Like western green mambas, they are tree dwellers that are active during the day. They eat birds and bats, as well as small rodents and lizards. They are shy snakes and will race to the treetops to escape danger. If they cannot get away from threats, such as humans, eagles, mongooses, and honey badgers, Jameson's mambas will strike repeatedly and fast. Their venom is deadly.

XTREME FACT – It is unknown where the name "Jameson's mamba" came from. Scottish zoologist Thomas Traill, who first wrote about the snake, may have named it after one of his college professors, Robert Jameson.

SNAKE HANDLERS

Most people never want to touch a mamba. But some people handle them in their work. Technicians "milk" venom from mambas. The venom is used to make antivenin to treat people who have been bitten. Police and wildlife removal experts are trained to capture and take away dangerous mambas. Herpetologists go to college to learn about reptiles and amphibians. They work for zoos and museums, as well as companies that do research and environmental studies.

A black mamba is milked for its venom. It is used to make antivenin. Only a few people have survived a mamba bite without this life-saving medicine.

IF YOU ARE BITTEN

If you are bitten by a mamba, it is important to follow these steps:

1) Get medical help IMMEDIATELY. Go right away, but walk. Get to a hospital as quickly as you can.

A researcher is bitten by a black mamba.

2) Stay calm. This keeps the heart from beating fast and spreading the venom quickly throughout the body.

3) Wrap a bandage tightly around the bite and up the limb that has been bitten. Keep the bitten area immobilized and below the heart. This helps slow the spread of the venom.

4) Get a good look or a photo of the snake so doctors know what type of snake it was and what antivenin to use.

 XTREME FACT – One black mamba has enough venom to kill 8 to 14 adults.

ARE THEY ENDANGERED?

Mambas are listed as "Least Concern" on the IUCN (International Union for Conservation of Nature) species list. Mambas prefer to stay away from humans. However, as humans move into their habitat, there is more contact between the deadly snakes and people.

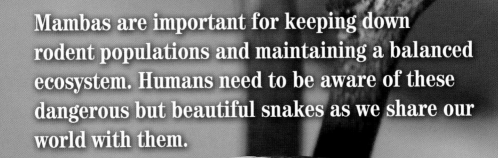

Mambas are important for keeping down rodent populations and maintaining a balanced ecosystem. Humans need to be aware of these dangerous but beautiful snakes as we share our world with them.

GLOSSARY

AMBUSH

A surprise attack by something hiding nearby.

ANTIVENIN

Also called antivenom. A liquid used to treat and stop the effects of a bite from venomous creatures, such as snakes. Antivenin is created by injecting an animal or eggs with a small amount of a specific snake's venom. The host animal produces antibodies against the venom, which can then be taken from its blood and used to treat humans.

BROOD

Babies that are all hatched or born at the same time.

CAMOUFLAGE

Coloring and/or physical appearance that allows a creature to blend in with its surroundings.

ECOSYSTEM

A biological community of animals, plants, and bacteria that live together in the same physical or chemical environment.

GENUS

A scientific category representing a group of living things that are all related to each other.

IMMOBILIZE

To prevent something, such as a hurt body part, from moving so no further damage happens, or in order for it to heal.

NEUROTOXIN

A substance, such as some snake venom, that attacks the victim's nervous system. Once injected into the body, a neurotoxin prevents the brain from sending messages to the rest of the body. A neurotoxin stops brain signals to the muscles. The body cannot move and the lungs cannot breathe. Death comes quickly.

PUPIL

The black part in the middle of the eye that opens and closes to let in more or less light. In most venomous snakes, the pupils are shaped like vertical slits. In mambas, the pupils are round.

RODENTS

Usually small mammals such as mice, rats, gerbils, hamsters, squirrels, and others with large front teeth. There are more rodents in the world than any other mammal group.

VENOM

A toxic liquid that some animals such as mambas, Gila monsters, and scorpions use for killing prey and for defense.

ONLINE RESOURCES

Booklinks
NONFICTION NETWORK
FREE! ONLINE NONFICTION RESOURCES

To learn more about mambas, visit abdobooklinks.com. These links are routinely monitored and updated to provide the most current information available.

INDEX